You HATE Computers, Admit It!

or
Our Love-Hate Relationships with Modern Technology and How to Fix Them

Bonus
Some Tips and Tricks You Will Really Like
Double Bonus
Some Quick Reference Cards
Triple Bonus
Reader Alerts, Checklists, and Some Step-by-Step Procedures

for Mac and PC Users and Phone Users
and Internet users and
Okay, okay. This book is for everybody!

BOB DEVANEY

PAGE PUBLISHING, INC.
New York, NY

First originally published by Page Publishing, Inc. 2018

We could not find the author of any of the images. If you have a copywrite to any of these, please let us know and we will remove them or acknowledge you, whichever you prefer.

ISBN 978-1-64424-363-3 (Paperback)
ISBN 978-1-64424-364-0 (Digital)

Printed in the United States of America

Contents

Introduction

Reader Alert: This book is *really boring*.

Correction: Given the subject matter, this book *could* be boring. So I have intermixed some things that I hope will "keep you in the game," as they say.

My attempt at humor (some of which has absolutely nothing to do with technology): My silly sense of humor is probably not "on the same page" as yours. But if it brings you one smile and keeps your head in this book, it will be worth it.

Included are the following :

- Tips and tricks
- Some hilarious pictures, starting with one in the next section
- Clarifying some weird terminology

How to read this book:

Procedure #1:

Read from cover to cover (as I have many times). Hopefully, you will pick up some nuggets of knowledge (teehee). Or you will pat yourself on the back and say, "Give me a break … I knew that already!" And yet, you will surely skip certain subjects that you currently have no interest in (e.g., "Create/change passwords").

Procedure #2:

Skim this like a comic book and just look at pictures and cartoons. Some of those will crack you up. I guarantee it!

Procedure #3

Skim for topics of interest.

Procedure #4

Use as a quick reference for specific topics in the table of contents and/or the index in the back.

Or

Combination of above (recommended). Start with procedure #2, then #3, and then #1.

No matter what you do, it is a very quick read even if you are a slow reader like me.

And if your friends and family really like this book, I could create a series of HATE books. ☺ For example,

- You Hate Your Job, Admit It
- You Hate Planes, Trains, and Automobiles, Admit It
- You Hate Hollywood, Admit It
- You Hate Politics, Admit It

And more!

Computers: You hate them or love them or both.
Internet: Ditto
Robo Calls: You flat-out hate them.
E-mails: I spend *way* too much time here. It is still a love/hate relationship
Facebook: Ditto

In this book, I will address all of the above. And I will toss in some tips and tricks that I hope will make your life in the tech world a little easier. And I will submit for you some "fixes" as well.

As a quick reference for any of the above, check out the Contents page and the index in the back of the book.

I hope you will have some fun along the way. So buckle up and let's get at it.

Computers

Well well well. We can't live with them, and we can't live without them.

In the interest of humor though, here are some country titles. The following has absolutely *nothing* to do with computers, but I can't help myself. If you don't have a sense of humor, just skip this section.

These are actual country western song titles.

- "Give Back My Heart" (Ya Big Ole Redneck Woman)
- "Won't You Ride in My Little Red Wagon" (cute)
- "Even Cowboys Like a Little Bit of Rock and Roll"

One reason I like "country" is that I can understand the words, and the lyrics are often a riot (as in the ones mentioned above).

Now, back to the business at hand …

Your computer and Smartphone as small as they are today, are more powerful than the computers of the late 1950s and early 1960s. And these massive machines took up a room the size of your first floor and were supported by tons of air-conditioning. These computers were called mainframes and are not part of my discussion in this book. Examples, however, can still be found at data centers like IBM, and the IRS. Gigantic, as you can imagine.

Fast-forward to today, and you see that there are two main types of computers for us "users," either PCs (Windows based) or Apple Macs.

Both of those come as either desktops, tablets, or laptops.

Pictures of Desktops

Pictures of Tablets

Pictures of Laptops

They all have their pluses and minuses. And I am not going to address those here. If you would like more information, go to the Internet (your "browser") and Google it. For example, in the Google search window, type:

"Difference between PC and Mac"
OR
"Difference between Windows and Mac OS"

As you know, Google is just *amazing*, huh?! It actually saved my life. I was feeling nauseous and had jaw pain one morning about 3:00 a.m. I have *never* experienced either. I went back to bed thinking I'll be okay in the morning; probably something I ate. Then I got to thinking, so I Googled those symptoms. Yikes. "Heart attack." The doc said, "It is a good thing you came in now [about 4:00 a.m.] 'cause you may have had the *big one* later." Also, he jokingly said, "You have a female heart as these are typical symptoms for females." Yikes again, nothing against females. I am just a full-blown male. Period.

So I wrote Google to thank them for saving my life. I was sure they would want me to be a poster child in their advertising. Hence, selfishly, I would become a millionaire. Noth'n, not even a form letter. But I (we) still love Google.

Okay. Enough about me.

Here are some (rather boring) definitions, but you have heard of most of them:

But first, consider all the work that your computer does for you: e-mail, documents, spreadsheets, photos, Internet … and the software that supports them. Since computers are electronic devices, they can only turn something on or turn something off. But they can do that very, *very* well. That "something" is call a bit. All of the above-mentioned activities boils down to simply 0s and 1s—all of your data and your software. Amazing, huh?

Bit: **B**inary dig**IT**; either a 0 or a 1.

RAM: **R**andom **A**ccess **M**emory. Well, you knew that
                 one.

Byte: 8 bits, one character

Nibble: Half a byte, 4 bits

Mega **B**yte (MB): 1 **Million B**ytes. 1,048,576 to be exact. Why such
                 an odd number? Well, glad you asked. Answer:

Because it is a power of 2. "What?" you say? Remember, the
computer can only work with 2 numbers (0 or 1), not 10 numbers like we humans. So 2 times 2 = 4x2 =8x2= 16x2= 32x2 = …
until you finally reach 1,048,576. Whew. Now, that was really,
really boring, huh?!

Giga **B**yte (GB): 1 billion bytes

Tera **B**yte (TB): 1 trillion bytes. Many new computers have at least
                 that much storage (disk space). *That* is a lot!

The Fix Is In (Well, Almost)

If your computer is stuck on stuff, just "boot" the booger (reference sidebar) if possible. But if able, be sure to save any files you have been working on. Restarting often resets everything to normal. If your computer is painfully slow, repeat the above.

If your computer is old (like me), take a nap. Oops. I got off track. Back up your data. You should do that regardless of the age … and often. This cannot be emphasized enough. I know from experience, sadly.

You *may* have to take it to the emergency room at your friendly retailer.

For Apple products, their store is just awesome. They have *always* been able to resolve whatever issue I have had. Ditto for your iPhone. Sometimes, they can resolve your issue when you walk in. But to be sure, make a reservation with their "Genius Bar."

Normal "Boot"/Restart:
1. Save your files.
2. Click on Start for PC. Click on Apple icon. For Mac users.
3. Click Restart.

Hard Boot (computer is locked up):
1. Hold the Start button down until the screen becomes dark.
2. Push Start button ("boot") to restart.

Technical Support: (800) MY–IPHONE (800–694–7466).

Or call a special store in your area. For Bethesda, Maryland, it's (301) 634-0880.

For Windows-based PCs, here are just a few tips:

- Microsoft finally has retail outlets at many malls.
- BestBuy has a Geek Squad as you may know. Phone: 800-433-5778
- Micro Center has technical support and a help desk at every store. Or you can call their help center at 614-850-3670
- In the Washington, DC, area, get to know BoonPC. You will have to take your computer into the store. His number is (301) 654-2116. He is really, really good and is reasonable often!! Note: I asked him for his first name, and he said, "Boon." So his full name is Boon Boon.

A Computer Checklist

- Back up your data and pictures
- Check your virus protection and scan your disk(s). Recommend Avast (free).
- Do *not* download unconfirmed files or open unconfirmed attachments.
- Password protect your computer.
- Delete temporary and obsolete files.
- Empty your Deleted Items folder.
- Defragment your disk(s).
- Purchase a surge protector with battery backup.
- Unplug your equipment during storms.
- Clean out your Inbox and folders.
- For more suggestions, Google "Computer checklist template."

My Favorite Tips

Don't know what to do?

On a PC: Right-click on it (i.e., position the mouse pointer in the area of interest like a picture and right-click in that area). A menu of options will be displayed.

On a MAC: Right-click on it. (If "Secondary Click" is enabled. If not, click on System Preferences, then Mouse, then Secondary Click.)

Example

Copy a picture from the Internet.

1. Position mouse pointer on top of picture.
2. Right-click (a menu will always appear).
3. Copy (then paste that wherever you would like (e.g., PowerPoint, Word, e-mail).

Try it! As Mikie would say, "Try it. You'll like it!"

Learn more about computers. Take one of Bob Devaney's courses. That's me. Well, that probably won't happen, sadly.

So there is a nice online tutorial you should look at, namely gcflearn-free.org/computerbasics/.

This website has a great set of selections:

Introduction

About This Tutorial

1.

What is a Computer?

2.

Hardware Basics

Basic Parts of a Computer

3.

Buttons and Ports on a Computer

4.

Inside a Computer

5.

Laptop Computers

6.

Mobile Devices

7.

Software Basics

Understanding Operating Systems

8.

Understanding Applications

9.

The Internet

The Internet is just an amazing resource, both good and bad. Don't you agree?!

First, the good.

Virtually *anything* you need to know is on the Internet, for example:

- Education – suffix ends in .EDU
  Elon.edu
  UMD.edu

- Government – suffix ends in .GOV
  FCC.GOV
  SSA.GOV
  USA.GOV

- Organizations, especially nonprofits – suffix ends in .ORG
  NEA.ORG
  REDCROSS.ORG

- Corporations – suffix ends in .COM
  IBM.COM
  AMAZON.COM
  GOOGLE.COM

And many more. Just Google "Internet domain suffixes" for a complete list.

Author's Note: Google, as you know, is a *very* popular software company and, hence, is considered a noun. But the website has been used *so* much that it is also considered a verb (an action item as in "Google this" or "Google that" or "Google your name," for example).

But please be very, *very* careful as some of these can be *extremely* bad as described in the next section. However, here are a few excellent resources

Health:	Mayo Clinic – MayoClinic.org
	Johns Hopkins Medicine – HopkinsMedicine.org
Research:	Google.com, of course. If you can't find what you want, it ain't there.
	The Library of Congress – LOC.gov
	The National Library of Medicine – NLM.NIH.GOV
Religion:	Your place of worship, for example:
	McLeanBible.org
	LDS.org
	Archdiocese of Washington – ADW.ORG

JewishEyes.org
IslamHouse.com

Travel: Travelocity.com
                 Hotel Search – Trivago.com

Entertainment: TV and Movies, HULU.COM

And now the bad, sometimes *very* bad. There are a number of sites that will infect your computer with a virus or worse. And some sex-related sites are certainly not fit for your kids … or anybody else for that matter.

The Fix

As a parent or guardian, you really want to protect your children from the evil that is out there. This is no place for them to learn about sex! Pornography is pervasive on the Internet. You should be rightfully concerned, and here are a few things you can do, if you haven't already.

In general, on your own computer, make sure that you password protect your account. Don't write it down and don't forget it! This should be for you and for you alone.

Here's how to password protect your account.

On a Mac

1.   Click on the apple icon in the upper left corner.
2.   Click System Preferences.
3.   Click on Security and Privacy in the first row.
4.   Under the General tab, click on Set Password.
5.   Fill in the blanks as prompted.
6.   Click Change Password.

On a PC

Windows 10

1. Click on the Start button (lower left corner).
2. Click on Settings icon (two up on the left side).
3. Click on Accounts (fourth row).
4. Click on Sign-in Options (left side).
5. Click Change (bottom right).
6. Fill in the blanks, as prompted.

Windows 7

1. Click on Start and then Control Panel.
2. Click on the User Accounts and Family Safety link.
3. Click on the User Accounts link.
4. In the Make changes to your user account area of the User Accounts window, click the Change your password link.

Then create one or more accounts for your children.

Here's the Procedure to create accounts for your children.

On a Mac

1. Click on the apple icon in the upper left corner.
2. Click System Preferences.
3. Click Users and Groups (fourth row).
4. Click the Lock icon lower left to unlock this window (you will be prompted to enter your password).
5. Click on the "+" sign just above the lock to add a new user.
6. Click on the arrows next to New Account.

7. Click Managed with Parental Controls.
8. Click arrows next to Age and click desired age.
9. Fill in the rest of this display and click Create User.
10. Enter password again when prompted
11. Click Open Parental Controls

Important Note: You can limit e-mails to just contacts and certain specific apps and websites. But there are too many "adult" (porn) sites to specify here. However, parental controls will *attempt* to avoid "adult" sites. You can also control the times that they will be allowed in their account.

We will deal with the adult sites again later.

Windows 10

1. Click the Windows icon (lower left corner of screen).
2. Select Settings (two icons up on the left side).
3. Tap Accounts (fourth row).
4. Select Family and other people.
5. Tap "Add someone else to this PC."
6. Continue as prompted.

Windows 7

1. To open User Accounts, click the Start button.
2. Click Manage another account.
3. Click Create a new account.
4. Type the name you want to give the user account, click an account type, and then click Create Account.

Viruses, Worms and Other Nasty Stuff

Virus: Some computer viruses are programmed to harm your computer by damaging programs, deleting files, or reformatting the hard drive. Even less harmful computer viruses can significantly disrupt your system's performance, sapping computer memory and causing frequent computer crashes.

Worm: A computer worm is a malicious, self-replicating software program (popularly termed as malware) that affects the functions of software and hardware programs. For example, it can also self-replicate itself and spread across networks. That is why worms are often referred to as viruses also.

Virus Protection: There is no need to buy expensive protection. Here are a couple for your consideration.

Microsoft Security Essentials: FREE.

Microsoft Security Essentials provides real-time protection for your home or small-business PC that guards against viruses, spyware, and other malicious software.

To install: Go to https://support.microsoft.com/en-us/help/14210/security-essentials-download.

Kind of a messy URL. Sorry. Or just Google "Microsoft Security Essentials." Or better yet, see Avast below, which is what I use.

Avast: FREE.

Avast Antivirus software has become one of the most popular choices to protect computers against malicious files. Available for free download as well as premium paid version, their software provides protection to a number of devices, including Windows, Mac, Android, and iOS. Even the free download version comes with multiple useful features, including virus and malware detection.

To install: Go to AVAST.COM.

Reader Alert: On the Internet or on Facebook, I recommend you *do not respond* to offers of free samples. True that they may be free, but you must pay S & H (shipping and handling). AHAAAAAA! There is the rub. Now that they have your credit card, you can count on additional monthly deliveries ($79.95, for example, on that credit card info that you gave them earlier). And the fine print of your order says that you are willing to accept addition shipments. Natch! Cancelling that order is borderline impossible. E-mail? Forget about it. They will, however, e-mail an order confirmation, but they will not reply to your request to cancel. A phone number is very hard to find. And if you do, they will give you a load of BS about how other folks like the product, blah blah blah. They make it impossible to cancel. (I've been trapped twice. Yes, I am a *very* slow learner.) As you probably know from experience, there are some very bad banditos out there.

The Fix: Visa and others, of course, are *very* helpful, and they will honor your "contested" charge(s).

Some More Definitions

What in the hey is a *cookie?* Wrong, this one is not eatable.

They are little files that hide in your computer so that your browser and websites can track your browsing sessions and save certain useful information, such as account names and passwords.

WWW: Answer provided in a subsequent quiz.

HTTPS: Answer also provided in a subsequent quiz.

URL: **U**ser **R**esource **L**ocator; the fancy name for a website. Example: WWW.UPS.COM

Note: The WWW is no longer required and the URL is not case sensitive, unlike passwords.

BLOG: We**B LOG**, a regularly updated website or web page, typically one run by an individual or small group that is written in an informal or conversational style on their topics of interest, often politics.

ISP: **I**nternet **S**ervice **P**rovider

BROWSER: Free software that is included with your computer and mobile devices. It lets you view web pages on the Internet, graphics, and most online content. Examples are Internet Explorer (IE), Chrome, Firefox, Safari and others.

WEB PAGE: A document (you may want to ignore the following Geek speak) commonly written in hypertext markup language (HTML) that is accessible through the Internet or other network using an Internet browser. A web page is accessed by entering a URL address (e.g., Google.com) and may contain text, graphics, and hyperlinks to other web pages and files.

Learn more about the internet. There is another on-line tutorial you should look at, namely gcflearnfree.org/basics/

This website also has a great set of selections.

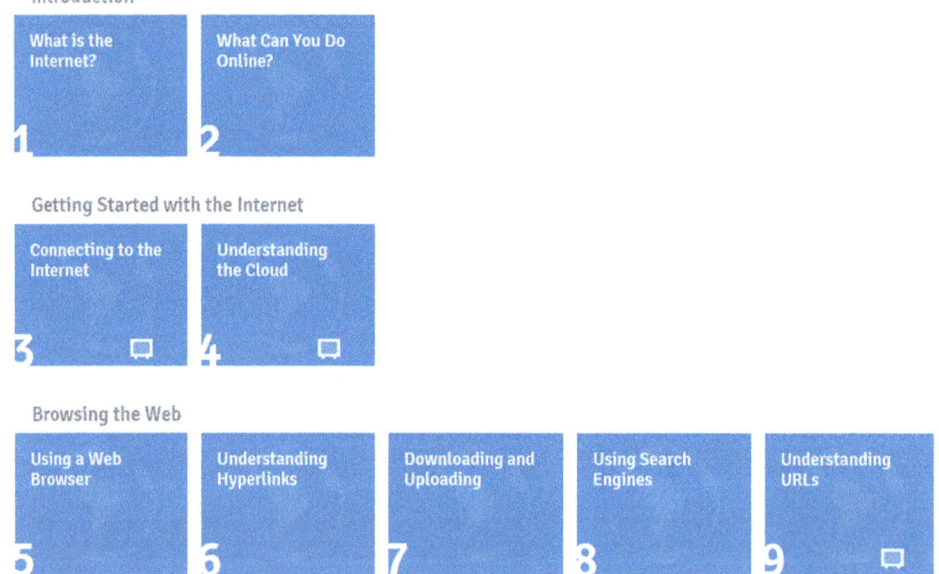

Phones

There are two general types of phones:

- Landline phones

If you remember this one, you may be older than me.

- Mobile phones. Many folks are dropping their landlines to save a few bucks (myself included) and because we usually have our mobile phones with us all the time—another excuse not to get up and answer the phone. Yes, I am lazy! Are you? (Be honest!)

But you knew that already. And there are two types of mobile phones:

- Flip phone(dumb—because it has no memory, basically, and no computer).

- Smart phone (smart—because it does have memory and a computer). However, they are getting rather pricey, more than many desktop computers. There are two main players in this arena. One begins with an *i* and the other with an *S*. What are they?

iPhone:

Samsung Smart Phone:

Robo Calls

Robo is short for *robotic* because a kazillion calls are generated by computers. A-ha, one reason you "hate" computers, I suppose. In the beginning, such calls were made by a live person (don't say it … we do not wish anyone dead). Then by prerecorded calls. Now, a computer simply selects from an electronic list and makes the call. They can now call a *lot* of people *fast*.

Again, *yikes*! We *all* just hate them. Agree?! Of course you do …

A little background music please: *all* robo-calls are *illegal*. There are a whole *lot* of companies committing crimes, huh?! As of 2017, it is estimated that almost two billion robo-calls were placed every single month. That is a bah-bah *B* like in *b*illion. Wow! Hence the hatred. It is actually the numero uno complaint received by the Federal Trade

Commission (FTC). And they receive over twenty thousand complaints *per day*! Sha-zaaam! And these are just the folks who are angry enough to call in the first place. You and I are probably not one of them, but we are mighty angry. *Grrrrrrrr.*

The ban on robo-calls has had no effect essentially. Good grief, you say; a whole lot of fluff about nothing, huh?!

Here are a couple of scenarios that you can certainly relate to:

Scenario #1: You are preparing dinner for your awesome family and as Lily Tomlin would say, "One ringy dingy … two ringy dingy." You pick up the phone, and (s)he says, "Is this the party with whom I am speaking?" *Robo!*

Your response: You either hang up or say, "Put me on your no-call list," which means they will do nothing. That does not scare anybody anymore. And do not press any numbers … just *hang up.*

What I did one time: I hung up a little too fast, and *he called me back*! Oops! He said, "Here is what it sounds like." *Bang.* Now, I am starting to feel a little bad; not too much, just a little.

What I *now* do: As soon as I realize that this is a sales pitch, I interrupt and say, "Listen, I know you are just trying to make an honest living [by this time, they have already hung up], but just put me on your no-call list [as you already know, that has little or no effect— more about that later]. Good day." And hang up.

Scenario #2: You just got home from work, and you are enjoying happy hour with your main squeeze, and the phone rings.

Your response: Don't answer it. If it is that important (e.g., a relative), they will leave a message. Or if it is really important, they will text you.

What I do: Look at the caller ID. If I do not recognize the number, I don't answer it. Your TV can most likely be set up to display that incoming caller ID.

Play Time: If you want to have some fun (and make money, perhaps—see below), play along with them until they finish their pitch. Gather as much information as you can. Ask for their name and the name of the company they represent. This is where they will probably get a little evasive. At the end of it all, just say, "You are awesome. Good day" and hang up. And make sure you note their phone number.

Now, sue them! *Seriously*! They will likely settle for at least $500 rather than the expense of litigation. It would be best if a letter is sent under your lawyer's letterhead.

Quiz: Do you know what "WWW" stands for?

> Correct. It stands for "world wide web."

Advanced Quiz: Do you know what "HTTPS" stands for? If you know the answer to this, then there is no need to read any further … 'cause you know it all.

> Correct. It stands for "HyperText Transport Protocol Secure," whatever that means (teehee). Look it up. You know, Google it.

Reader Alerts:

- Fake IRS calls. The real IRS will *never* call you; always by mail.
- "This is Microsoft calling, and your computer is in grave danger." Or some such. As with the IRS, they will never make a call like this.
- Phony offers.
- Call "spoofing." These are fake phone numbers that may seem to be that of a friend; also, a popular e-mail spoof.
- So-called "friends" who claim to be out of the country and asking for money because they have lost all ID, cash, and credit cards. Again, this is most prevalent on e-mails. Sadly, there are gullible folks who have a big heart and fall for this disturbing stuff. Grrrrrrrrrr.
  "If it sounds too good to be true, it probably is."

BTW ("by the way" for non-texters), if you want a complete list, Google "Texting abbreviations" (e.g., ROFL = Rolling On the Floor Laughing).

The Fix (Well, Almost)

You can add your number(s) to the "Do Not Call Registry" with the Federal Trade Commission (FTC). *But nothing actually happens.* What, you say? Nothing prevents the solicitor from calling you. They probably don't even have a "do not call" list. It *may* give you some recourse if enough complaints are received by the FTC about the particular number that called you.

Bottom Line: The so-called no-call list does not work. Geez, a whole lot of smoke and no fire. The FTC has prepared lawsuits against just over thirty companies. They simply do not have enough lawyers to litigate these cases.

If makes you feel any better, however, go ahead and register.

Procedure: Call 888-38-1222 from the phone you want to register.

Or on the Internet, you can do the following (you can enter up to three phone numbers from here):

1. Go to "WWW.DONOTCALL.GOV."
   or simply DONOTCALL.GOV.
2. Click on "Register Your Phone."
3. Click "REGISTER HERE."
4. Follow the instructions from there.
5. Click, "SUBMIT."

Or on the Internet, go to "FCC.GOV."

If you are a Verizon user, they *may* display the word "SPAM" on your caller ID if they suspect it is a solicitation. Yeah. Thank you, Verizon!

Other types of organizations may still call you, such as charities, political groups, debt collectors, and surveys. And you will still get marketing calls, as you all know.

Now what?

On an iPhone:

To block a particular robo call or any caller for that matter:

1. Click on your phone icon.
2. Click on Recents (at the bottom).
3. Click on the "i" to the right of that number.
4. Scroll down and click Block this Caller.

Tip: Zooming (increase or decrease the screen size). This is especially handy on the Internet where the point size can be very small. Or you are projecting something on the screen for your audience and the folks in the back cannot see it (e.g., an Excel spreadsheet).

Procedure:

ON A PC: Do a "Control Roll."

Okay, Bob, what in the heck are you talking about?! Hold down the CTRL key while moving the roller on top of your mouse back and forth.

Or if you don't have a mouse, hold down the CTRL key and touch the "+" or "-" keys one or more times.

On a Mac: Hold down ALT+COMMAND, then click on the "+" or "–" keys one or more times.

E-Mails

So, is your face in your Inbox most of your day? Stop it! Really!

Your *time management* needs work. Most of us are guilty of this problem, including myself. But I finally, *finally* realized that I sure have more important things to do. Consider the countless hours we waste just staring at our e-mails … and waiting patiently for more. Are you sitting all day just checking and responding to e-mails? Not good. So at the end of the day, ask yourself, "What have I really accomplished?!"

The Fix (Almost)

First of all, for your own health, you have *got* to get your arse out of that chair every thirty minutes. Set an alarm (see below) if you must. And furthermore, remember the following:

*   When you are sitting, make sure the monitor is at eye level. Otherwise, you are straining your neck and your back.
*   Sit up straight with your shoulders back.
*   Take a breath once in a while—a *deep* one.
*   Drink water … often! You are probably dehydrated.

Set your alarm: On your iPhone, click Utilities. Click on your Clock, then Timer. Adjust the time to thirty minutes. Then hit Start. When the alarm goes off, get up and walk around and drink a glass of water while you are at it. Then click on Repeat. Nice.

TIP: Rest your mouse (and wrists)

There are many times when you don't have to grab your mouse and position the pointer to a desired location.

1.   Use the Enter key:

     * If you see "OK," press Enter
     * "Save"
     * "Print"
     * After you type your password when prompted, press Enter

2.   Use the Esc key:

     * If you see "Cancel," press Esc.
     * To close an e-mail, press Esc.

Here is the fix, or "here is the plan, man."

First of all, you do *not* have to respond to every *ding* that says, "You have mail!" If it is that important, they will either call you or text you. You might consider turning off your volume so that you are *not* tempted.

If you don't need your computer for other work, go somewhere else. I actually go to another room with my laptop. Set time slots for reading your e-mails. For example:

1. First thing in the morning
2. After lunch,
3. Close of business (COB).

The rest of the time you will have available to "git'r done," as Larry the Cable Guy would say. Please try this and note how much more productive you are.

Some More Definitions

SPAM: Unsolicited messages (such as e-mails, text messages, or Internet postings) sent to a large number of recipients or posted in a large number of places.

PHISHING: "Gone fish'n." Not really, but you knew I had to do that. *Sorry*. Getting serious, it is the fraudulent practice of sending e-mails purporting to be from reputable companies in order to induce individuals to reveal personal information, such as passwords and credit card numbers.

SPOOF: A technique used to gain unauthorized access to computers, whereby the intruder sends messages to a computer indicating that the message is coming from a trusted host (e.g., a friend).

Other Issues

Tip: The following is beyond tedious. So if this does not apply to you for the moment, skip to the next section, "Messaging Applications."

Dealing with "Junk" Mail

Such a pesky problem and so many solutions. But nothing is fool-proof. Check your Spam and Junk mail folders often as some legitimate e-mail may be in there.

First of all, moving an e-mail to your Junk folder should prevent that sender from entering your Inbox in the future.

On a Mac, enable junk mail filtering:

1. While you are in Apple Mail, click on Mail (top left).
2. Click on Preferences.
3. Click Junk Mail button (third from left).
4. Click Enable junk mail filtering.
5. Click Reset button.

On a PC for Microsoft (often abbreviated as MS) Outlook:

1. In the Home tab, click on Junk (in the Delete group)
2. You can "block" this particular sender. Or click Junk Email Options and pick a general rule to follow in the future, like move obvious junk mail to the junk e-mail folder.

Searching for Old E-Mails

On the Mac:

1. Click in the Search window.
2. Type all or part of the desired name.
3. Press Enter.

On the PC: There are so many e-mail providers that I can only say to look for a search box and repeat from above. However, the most common software is GMAIL. In this case, do this:

1. At the top of your email list, click on Search.
2. Type desired text.
3. Press Enter.

Cleaning up Your Inbox

- Delete one at a time. Yikes.

    o For just a few e-mails, click on each one and press Delete key.

- Select many unwanted e-mails and then delete. This can go quickly (this is what I do every morning).

    o While holding down the CTRL key, click desired e-mails and then delete.
    On a Mac, hold down the command key and repeat above.

- Select a block of e-mails and delete. Very fast.

    o Click on the first e-mail in the block.
    o Hold down the Shift key and click the last e-mail in desired block. Then, delete.

- Use a "filter" to automatically select certain e-mails and then delete.

  o In Outlook, there is a Filter E-mail under the Home tab.
  o On a Mac, create a "rule."

    - Click Mail (top left)
    - Click Preferences
    - Click Rules button (far right)
    - Click Add Rule
    - Select desired options (e.g., any recipient that contains "politics")
    - Move message to Trash (for example)

- Delete everything (probably not)

  o Hold down the CTRL key and press A (for all) and then delete
    On a Mac, hold down the command button and touch A

- Finally, you need to empty your "trash" folder.

Learn More about Email: There is a nice on-line tutorial you should look at: getlearnfree.org/emailbasics /introduction-to-email/1/.

Messaging Applications

Instant Message (IM)

With IM, you can text people you interact with, and they receive it *immediately* using their mobile or cell phone numbers. And it is a nice way for parents to keep in touch with their children. You can IM with anyone on your buddy list or contact list. You type messages to each other into a small window that shows up on both of your screens.

Most IM programs provide these features:

Instant messages - Send notes back and forth with a friend who is online
Chat - Create a chat room with friends or co-workers
Web links - Share links to your favorite websites
Video - Send and view videos and chat face-to-face with friends
Images - Look at an image stored on your friend's computer
Sounds - Play sounds for your friends
Files - Share files by sending them directly to your friends
Talk - Use the Internet instead of a phone to actually talk with friends
Streaming content - Real-time or near-real-time stock quotes and news
Mobile capabilities - Send instant messages from your cell phone

Twitter

Twitter is an online news and social networking site where people communicate in short messages called tweets. Tweeting is sending short messages to anyone who follows you on Twitter, with the hope that your messages are useful and interesting to someone in your audience.

Instagram

Instagram is a mobile, desktop, and Internet-based photo-sharing application and service that allows users to share pictures and videos either publicly or privately to preapproved followers.

Snapchat

Snapchat is a photo-sharing app that changes privacy norms in a very novel way. The free app allows users to send others photos and control how long receivers can see them. These photos last for up to ten seconds before they disappear forever.

Facebook

Again, like Google, this is an excellent resource for many things, especially information and pictures about our families.

But how do we block so many posts and ads that we don't care about?

To no longer allow posts from a particular friend:

1. Go to that friend's timeline (search for friend).
2. Move the mouse pointer to Following.
3. Click Unfollow.

You should no longer see this friend's updates on your news feed. You can still see their updates if you visit their profile/timeline page.

To block other posts:

1. Click on the ellipsis (. . .) in the upper right of that post.
2. Click Hide post or, if listed, click Unfollow.

Learn More about Email: There is still another on-line tutorial you should look at, namely

Go to: gcflearnfree.org/facebook101/.

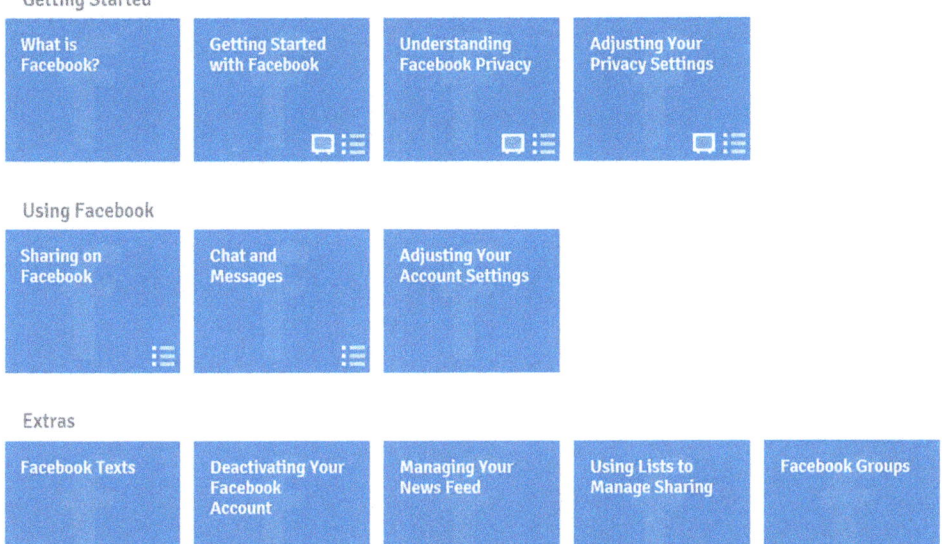

Conclusion

I do hope you managed to smile along the way. But more importantly, I hope you picked up a thing or three that you can use to your benefit! Certainly, this was not meant to be an exhaustive manuscript on these subjects lest it be too tedious and boring. Wake up, I tell you!

If this book did not address your specific issues. I am sorry. But you already know the fix … "Google it." It has never failed me. In fact, much of the research for this book was accomplished with Google. And best of all, it saved my life in 2010, as I mentioned before. Can't ask for more than *that*.

As for me, I *love* computers. (Well, it has put bread on my table for many moons as I am a Microsoft Office trainer … and I *love* doing that).

Before you leave …

Homework

When was the last time you were given a homework assignment?! For me, that would be measured in decades, not years.

1. Check out my website ... I'm beg'n ya.

    MicrosoftOfficeTraining.US.COM

2. E-mail me about your impression of this book, positive or negative. That would mean a lot to me and my publisher, Page Publishing.

    BobDevaney@GMAIL.COM

3. Check out the list of courses that I teach in appendix A.

Well, that's it. Thanks for being an important part of my first book. Appreciate it! See you again, I hope.

Acknowledgments

My wife, Jo Ann, of fifty-nine years. She had absolutely no input into this book. In fact, she did not even know I was writing it until I sent it to the publisher. But her love is all I needed to motivate me. CORRECTION She actually had a LOT of input after I received edits from my publisher. Thanks, Honey!! This would not have worked without you!

My family: Ditto as with my wife. But I do have the best family a person could even imagine. Don't doubt me on that!

My friends. Ditto as my family above.

My Lord and Savior, Jesus Christ.

Page Publishing and especially Casey Runyan, Literary Development Agent for keeping me focused and Kelly Crum, my Publish Coordinator. The process has been a joyful one!

Appendices

Appendix A

Courses Taught by Bob

Subject List:

Email me for customized courses (Microsoft Office 2003, 2007, 2010, 2013, or 365).

Contact me for course descriptions (basic and advanced).

Private Tutoring and Consulting, as needed

* Browsers: Just the Basics (and Other Goodies)
* Excel: Just the Basics
* Excel: Some Advanced Considerations, Including Tips and Tricks
* Excel: Formulas and Functions
* Excel: Database Applications (Sort, Filter, Subtotals, and more)
* Excel: Summarizing and Analyzing Data with Pivot Tables
* Excel: Charting and Graphics
* Excel: Linking—within Spreadsheets and to Other Applications
* Exploring Windows Explorer (My Computer)
* Office 2007, 2010. 2013, 2016 or 365, Jumpstart (What's new and what's different)
* OneNote
* Outlook: Tips and Tricks for Experienced Users
* Outlook: Calendars/Appointments, Contacts, and Tasks

* Outlook: Meetings and Events, an In-Depth Look
* Outlook: Vote Casting and Tallying Results
* Outlook: Tasks—Assigning, Controlling, and Monitoring
* Outlook: Sharing—Calendars, Mail, and Others
* PowerPoint: Just the Basics
* PowerPoint: Some Advanced Considerations, Including Tips and Tricks
* PowerPoint: Charting, Drawing, and Working with Objects
* PowerPoint: Animation—Graphics, Audio, Video
* Tips to Enhance the Microsoft Office User: Selected Tips in Windows, Internet Explorer, Word, Excel, and PowerPoint
* Word: Tips and Tricks
* Word: Envelopes, Labels, and Mail Merge
* Word: Mastering Tables
* Word: Working with Large Documents; Table of Contents, Index, and More
* Word: Formatting Considerations: Styles, Templates, and More
* Word: Graphics and Drawing Objects
* Word: Document Review Cycle (Versions and Tracking Changes)

NOTE: The Office products can be presented in versions 2003, 2007, 2010, 2013, 2016 or 365.

Appendix B

Sample Quick Reference Card

Ask me to send you print versions of these files in MS Word. You could then print them, two-sided and in color, of course, and preferably on heavy-duty paper.

Quick Reference Cards:

- Office 365
- Excel
- Word
- PowerPoint
- OneNote
- Outlook
- Access

Sample Quick Reference Card

Popular Shortcuts - Quick Reference Card

Feature	Shortcut
GENERAL	
Copy	Ctrl + C
Cut	Ctrl + X
Paste	Ctrl + V
Undo	Ctrl + Z
Print (Dialog Box)	Ctrl + P
Open	Ctrl + O
Save	Ctrl + S
New (document, email message, workbook, etc.)	Ctrl + N
Select all (entire document, emails, files, etc.)	Ctrl + A
Zoom	Ctrl + "roll" (on your mouse)
Close Dialog Boxes (Cancel button). Close email message window.	Esc
Default Dialog buttons (Save, OK, Print, ...)	Enter
Select (with your keyboard)	Shift + arrow movement keys
Maximize a window	Double click the Title Bar
THE most important tip	Right-Click
WINDOWS	
Start Menu	Windows Logo key (between Ctrl & Alt)

Feature	Shortcut
Show/Restore Desktop (minimizes all windows)	Logo + D
Windows Explorer or "My Computer" (Windows XP) or "Computer" (Windows 7)	Logo + E
Lock (your screen)	Logo + L
Alternate Tasks (programs, windows)	Alt + Tab
Cascading Windows (Windows 7 only)	Logo + Tab
Windows Mobility Center (laptop controls for Windows 7 only)	Logo + X
INTERNET	
Address bar (in your Browser)	Alt + D
Organize your Favorites	Ctrl + B
Open New Tab (Internet window)	Ctrl + T

Feature	Shortcut
WORD	
Move one word at a time	Ctrl + Right arrow (or left arrow)
Move to end of line	End
Move to beginning of line	Home
Move to beginning of document	Ctrl + Home
Move to end of document	Ctrl + End
Move one page at a time (instead of one SCREEN at a time)	Ctrl + Page Down (or Page Up)
Select a word	Double click anywhere on word
Select a sentence	Ctrl + click anywhere in a sentence

Feature	Shortcut
Select a paragraph	Triple click anywhere in a paragraph
Select entire document	Ctrl + A
Center	Ctrl + E
Align left	Ctrl + L
Align right	Ctrl + R
New Page	Ctrl + Enter
New line (for entering blank lines between bullets or numbered lists)	Shift + Enter
Return to previous edit points (up to 3)	Shift + F5
Increase point size (after selecting text)	Ctrl + Shift + >
Decrease point size (after selecting text)	Ctrl + Shift + <
Bullets and numered lists: "demote" to next level	Tab
Bullets and numered lists: "promote" to previous level	Shift + Tab
EXCEL	
Switch between open spreadsheets	Ctrl + Page Down (or Page Up)
Cancel entry (especially if you accidently got into a formula)	Esc
Move to the right	Tab or right-arrow
Move to the left	Shift + Tab or left arrow
Move down	Enter or down arrow
Enter current date	Ctrl + ; (semi-colon)

Support and Training:

1. E-mail anytime. Your time is too valuable to be stuck on stuff. Your first call is free.
2. Classroom training and Webinars (one to three hours). Call for course descriptions and costs.
3. Check this website periodically for "What's New, Tips, and Did you Know that": MicrosoftOfficeTraining.US.COM.

Index

About the Author

Notice the loss of hair. Actually, we don't "lose" our hair. Part of the aging process is to suck the hair follicles back into our body and spit them out in other places like our ears and nose. UGH.

The following is excellent night time reading because you will fall asleep in one nanosecond.

I started at the Goddard Space Flight Center, as a Mathematician/ Programmer. I pinch myself now thinking about how much fun I had working on our first satellite, the Echo balloon, and later our manned Apollo program. In the process, I co-authored two papers in the area of celestial mechanics.

After 10 years, I was introduced to training. It was really REALLY terrifying for me at first as I was beyond shy as a youngster.

But, it became a career to this day because I like the technology and I love people.

Now, I am working on my first book; this one. And, with your support, I hope this is the first of many. I am surprised that I like writing as English was my worst subject in both High School and college. However, over the years, I have authored a number of user manuals, quick reference cards, and training materials.

On a personal side, I have been married to my bride for many moons and we have 3 **awesome** children and 7 **wonderful** GRAND children. They make me feel young(er). I fulfilled a lifetime dream and got my pilot's license at age 50. Oh my... I cannot even express the beauty and thrill of it all. I have a very long "bucket list."

Author's note: would somebody just pinch me?!!!! THE luckiest man in the world. (That's me.)
Bob Devaney, Microsoft Office Trainer
BobDevaney@gmail.com
Kensington, MD

www.ingramcontent.com/pod-product-compliance
Lightning Source LLC
Chambersburg PA
CBHW040110180526
45172CB00009B/1289